Yurlmun
Mokare Mia Boodja

'Returning to Mokare's Home Country'
Encounters and Collections in Menang Country

Welcome

Kaia Kooliny, Yoor-al mia Boodja,
Nidja mia Noongar Boodja
mia Menang yunga

Hello you come here to our home Country
This place is Noongar land,
home of the Menang people

We acknowledge and celebrate the First Australians
on whose traditional lands we come together.
We pay our respects to our elders past and present.

Please be advised that this publication contains
the names and images of people who are now deceased.

Contents

A note on spelling

Menang leader Mokare's name has been spelt variously in historical and contemporary accounts:
for example, 'Mawcarri', 'Markew', 'Mokaré', 'Mokaré' and 'Mokkare'. Noongar is spelt as 'Noongar',
'Nyungar', 'Nyoongar', 'Nyoongah', 'Nyungah', 'Nyugah', 'Nyungar', 'Yungar' and 'Noonga'. Menang
also appears as 'Minang'. In accordance with current Menang people's usage, these words are spelt
'Mokare', 'Noongar' and 'Menang' in this publication.

Foreword

Hon. John Day MLA

Minister, Culture and the Arts

It is a pleasure to provide a foreword to this publication which accompanies the unique exhibition at Western Australian Museum's Albany site.

Yurlmun: Mokare Mia Boodja provides a powerful example of the Museum's commitment to regional Western Australia and to providing opportunities for everyone in our State to share stories about their past, present and future.

The exhibition is also a product of the strong partnership that the Museum has built with the National Museum of Australia in Canberra and, over the last five years, with the British Museum. Those two great national museums worked for many years to create the recent ground-breaking exhibitions, *Indigenous Australia: Enduring Civilisation*, in London, and *Encounters: Revealing Stories of Aboriginal and Torres Strait Islander Objects from the British Museum*, at the National Museum of Australia in Canberra. *Yurlmun: Mokare Mia Boodja* is, in many ways, only possible because of the groundwork that underpinned these two exhibitions.

The determination, hard work and dedication of the Albany Heritage Reference Group Aboriginal Corporation and the broader Menang community were also crucial to the development of the exhibition.

The extensive engagement between the Menang people of the region and the staff of the British Museum is unprecedented and has led to renewed conversations and a deeper understanding of the nature and significance of cultural material.

The productive dialogue that has led to the co-curation of this exhibition, will hopefully, provide the basis for future conversations and collaborations between museums and indigenous communities in Australia and throughout the world.

This publication explores the relationships between Menang people and early colonists. In particular, it considers the special relationship between Menang leader Mokare and surgeon and Government Resident Dr Alexander Collie. Importantly, it says as much about our present as it does about our past, and the final chapter provides a fascinating insight into the journey that led to the return of these objects to Country and the significance of this event to Menang people.

I congratulate everyone involved in this very significant collaboration, the power of which is not only in the objects presented but in the conversations that will emerge from it.

Foreword

Alec Coles

CEO, Western Australian Museum

Museums should be places where people can share their stories without fear or favour. They are the archetypal 'safe places for unsafe ideas', to quote the oft-repeated phrase that I believe was first coined by the great cultural commentator Elaine Heumann Gurian. Those stories can be inspirational and uplifting but can equally be challenging and confronting; those that deal with the relationship between early European arrivals and Australia's first peoples are inevitably complex and influenced, absolutely, by perspective.

It is for these reasons that I am so pleased that the Western Australian Museum has been able to work with the Menang community to bring objects from the British Museum collections back to Country for this important exhibition, and to share and explore the stories that surround them.

These 14 objects represent, not only the everyday items of Menang people at the time, but also powerful expressions of culture and Country. Over decades, they have become imbued with even greater significance as they sit at the centre of discussions and debates around ideas of exchange and appropriation; of partnership and subjugation; of friendship and expediency; and of colonisation and invasion.

On behalf of the Western Australian Museum, I would like to take this opportunity to thank our many partners in this project: in particular, the Albany Heritage Reference Group Aboriginal Corporation (AHRGAC); the British Museum; the National Museum of Australia; the Department of Aboriginal Affairs (DAA); the City of Albany; and the Great Southern Development Commission.

Particular thanks are due to Vernice Gillies of the AHRGAC, Harley Coyne of the DAA, Gaye Sculthorpe at the British Museum, and Mat Trinca and Ian Coates at the National Museum of Australia. I also would like to thank all the Western Australian Museum staff, both in Albany and Perth, who have contributed to *Yurlmun: Mokare Mia Boodja*.

I hope that the journey home to Country of these 14 objects is a momentous and affirming event for Menang people. I also hope that it contributes to a vibrant discussion about the role of museums, about the nature of collections and about issues of cultural expression, exchange, ownership and appropriation.

Fig. 1   Statue of Mokare, which stands in a park off the main street of the City of Albany. It was erected on 18 April 1997, as a community project, in recognition of the role he played in the peaceful co-existence between Noongar people and the first European settlers, and in conjunction with the Noongar community, Department of Aboriginal Affairs and the City of Albany.

Courtesy Laurie Benson

Preface

Vernice Gillies
Chairperson, AHRGAC

Yurlmun: Mokare Mia Boodja

These Menang words mean 'Returning to Mokare's Home Country'. This one-off exhibition at the Western Australian Museum in Albany is a celebration, not only of the objects coming home, but also of the unique and very special relationship formed in the 1800s between Menang leader Mokare and colonist Alexander Collie. Mokare became his trusted guide and close friend. So strong was the trust and friendship that Collie wished to be buried next to Mokare. The objects in this exhibition reflect this close relationship.

The Albany Heritage Reference Group Aboriginal Corporation (AHRGAC) has worked in partnership with the Western Australian Museum, and with the support and cooperation of the British Museum and the National Museum of Australia to bring our 14 King George Sound objects back to Menang Country, whence they originated. To have achieved this in the extremely limited time we had available has meant a lot of juggling, hard work and persistence. But it paid off.

We are privileged that the Menang community is able to display these very old artefacts on our (and their) homelands. We believe this is a unique event in Australian history, and it is also the first time that the British Museum has helped to arrange a display of such objects in the originating Country, in Australia.

Without a lot of hard work and dedication from all of our partners, it could not have happened. To describe what this exhibition means to our community is difficult because it will mean different things to different people. We feel enjoyment, pride, connection – and maybe some sadness – that they will return to London. So we will enjoy them while we have them at home.

We sincerely hope that other Aboriginal communities around Australia will also be afforded the privilege of one day sharing their precious objects with their own people, just as we have been lucky enough to do.

The AHRGAC acknowledges the generous support of the Western Australian Museum (WAM), the British Museum, the National Museum of Australia, the Department of Aboriginal Affairs (DAA), the City of Albany and our wonderful emerging leaders from Follow the Dream, Albany.

Our special thanks to Harley Coyne and Robert Reynolds from DAA, James Dexter, Ross Chadwick, Tanya Edwards and Matt Britton from WAM, and a big 'thank you' to Gaye Sculthorpe of the British Museum and the hard-working members of the AHRGAC Steering Committee. None of this would have happened if we had not been able to work together.

Introduction

Gaye Sculthorpe and Maria Nugent

Objects provide occasions. They provide occasions for the telling of stories, for learning and sharing knowledge, for the honouring of ancestors, and for remembering, celebrating and grieving. When objects that have long been held in museums are brought out of storage and returned to their places of origin, new opportunities open up for delving into the contexts from which they came and through which they travelled, and for gaining insights into the meanings and associations they acquired along the way. Every object is a product of multiple and overlapping histories – and so there are many stories to be told. This publication tells some of the histories and stories surrounding 14 objects from King George Sound that returned to Country for the *Yurlmun: Mokare Mia Boodja* exhibition.

The southwest of Western Australia around Albany belongs to the Menang, and they belong to it. Their Ancestral stories and songs tell of their relationship to the Country and sustain their custodianship of it. They have been in this place for thousands of years. Beginning only a few hundred years ago, the Menang became increasingly accustomed to dealing with 'men from over the ocean's horizon' as European and American voyagers, sailors and whalers sailed past their shores and into their harbours.[1]

By the 1820s, a small contingent of British men and women had become resident among them. In this small shared space, and for a brief time, friendships were forged, new social worlds were created, and words, things, technologies and ideas were exchanged. The essays offered here describe that world: the changing contexts in which the objects the Menang made – and the knowledge they possessed – moved into the hands and heads of Europeans, and began to circulate through new networks and into other, often distant, domains.

The volume begins in the summer of 1821–22 with Tiffany Shellam's essay describing how Menang sought to satisfy the demand for artefacts by Phillip Parker King's expedition, with ship's biscuits becoming the local currency. From there, Daniel Simpson's essay discusses Alexander Collie's collecting in the 1830s for the Royal Navy's Haslar Hospital Museum, outlining the wider imperial context of collecting and insights into Collie's and his colleagues' values, ambitions and motivations. The essay by Ian Coates and Alison Wishart complements this discussion by describing how Collie's botanical collecting was facilitated by close connections with Menang men, particularly Mokare, who shared their knowledge of Country with him. Gaye Sculthorpe's contribution reminds us that objects were often acquired through more fleeting encounters, such as during shipping stopovers at Albany.

*It's important that things like these here are displayed
and shown and talked about so that people do understand …
where we are coming from and how long we have been here.*

Ezzard Flowers, Menang Elder, 2012

Objects were bought as mementoes of travels, or as additions to larger collections already assembled. However, few local residents made collections. Murray Arnold's essay suggests why that may have been so. He describes the changing relations between Menang and colonists and settlers during the nineteenth century. Like other contributors, he notes the friendly relations that reigned during the garrison period, but which began to fracture when the area was opened up to 'free' settlement and new arrivals began increasingly to behave as though they owned the place.

Throughout the various essays in this volume, we learn more about the objects themselves, including the species of wood from which they were made, as identified by Caroline Cartwright. Harley Coyne and John Carty's essay provides a powerful reminder about the work that old objects can do in new contexts. They bring the discussion into the present by telling the story of the Menang people's appeal to the British Museum to have their objects come back on Country. In the process of telling this story, they illustrate the ways in which these objects continue to mediate relationships between people and institutions, just as they had in the past. Their essay brings past and present into dialogue in inspiring ways.

Like most such institutions, the British Museum and the Western Australian Museum take seriously the responsibility to research and interpret their collections, and to provide accurate and authoritative information about the objects for which they are the custodians. They seek to make that knowledge widely accessible, but also in ways that respect the views and desires of the communities whose material heritage they hold.

This publication is part of that commitment. Our hope is that the information and insights offered by the authors will contribute to the sharing of knowledge about the Menang objects in the British Museum and the histories they hold. We recognise that this is only one aspect of the ongoing work of interpretation and knowledge production. The exhibition of the objects on Menang Country will generate many more memories, histories, stories and interpretations, and we look forward to having our own understandings enriched as a result.

Chapter One

'Thro' the medium of biscuits'
Phillip Parker King and the Menang, 1821

Tiffany Shellam

From 1791, the Menang Noongar experienced over three decades of encounters with European voyagers before a British garrison settlement was set up on their Country in 1826, a military outpost of New South Wales. They had watched Captain George Vancouver's ship from a distance in 1791 and by the time they met with Matthew Flinders in December 1801, during which time one old man participated in a military drill on the beach, the Menang had also encountered American and English sealers and whalers. In 1803 Nicolas Baudin's French scientific expedition had visited their shores too. These encounters with English, French and American visitors meant that the Menang accumulated varied experiences of interactions with strangers of different kinds who came in ships and engaged with them in trade.

Lieutenant Phillip Parker King was instructed by the Admiralty and the Colonial Office to fill in the gaps of Flinders' earlier survey. Between 1818 and 1822 he visited King George Sound on three separate occasions. However, it was not until December 1821, on his second visit, in the *Bathurst*, that he and his crew met with the Menang. On this visit King stayed for ten days in Oyster Harbour, which allowed for an intimate and prolonged encounter that revolved around intense daily trade: the explorers were eager to collect Aboriginal curiosities, the Menang were keen for ship's biscuit. King's published journals contained his accounts of the Menang as a 'fearless' and 'friendly' people who were eager to trade.

Wirlomin Noongar novelist Kim Scott has suggested that in this era Menang Noongar were a community so confident of their place in the world that they welcomed the new: 'they were hospitable and generous landlords at that, curious about new cultural "devices" and cross-culturally competent enough to display the "habits" of the other in the interests of cross-cultural communication'.[2] The openness of the Menang and their willingness to engage in barter with visitors is the theme of this chapter.

On 23 December 1821, King's expedition entered King George Sound, and with his botanist, Allan Cunningham, King rowed towards the entrance of Princess Royal Harbour in a boat. Nine Menang men waded out to meet them, welcoming these strangers to their Country. Cunningham and King threw them some salt beef and ship's biscuit; they ate the biscuit with 'apparent thankful spirit', the taste for it, Cunningham thought, they had 'already acquired by having previously eaten it'.[3] Once securely anchored in the adjacent Oyster Harbour, interviews began. Cunningham captured a sense of Menang openness and experience:

> … *upon our boat landing … two of them eagerly jumped into it and took a passage on board showing us most satisfactorily that they knew what it was to be on shipboard … that they had been on board other vessels … They jumped on our boat with … liveliness of joy, which is usually manifested upon meeting old esteemed friends, and altho' they were fully aware they had thrown themselves within the power of strangers, they exhibited the most cheerful disposition, surrounding us with their songs, the subject of which seem'd to be on the objects around them.*[4]

The two Menang men were rowed to the *Bathurst*, where they were each clothed in a pair of sailor's trousers. Another man was also taken on board and stayed all day, participating in transactions. According to Cunningham, this man was 'very, very comfortable, for our people had shav'd him and given him tea; and so much did he enter into the enjoyment of such luxuries, that scarcely the light of his anxious countrymen on the beach, or our own solicitations could induce him to allow us to land him'.[5]

We were the first ones to make 'contact' in this area and I'm immensely proud that my ancestors established a peaceful approach to the relationship they built with the incomers.

Lester Coyne, Menang Elder, 2016

He was, Cunningham thought, 'truly remarkable for his mild manners, great native intelligence, and special communicative dispositions, and so much had he engaged the esteem of Lt King' and the crew that they gave him 'the hackneyed name of Jack, to which title he soon answered on all occasions'.[6] King also ordered special treatment for Jack. 'The natives,' he wrote, 'were not permitted to come on board until 4 o'clock in the afternoon, excepting Jack', who came and went as he pleased.[7]

The *Bathurst* was anchored in the narrow entrance to Oyster Harbour for the duration of the expedition's visit, with groups of Menang assembled on the opposite shores. Every day groups from each shore took turns at being taken out to the brig. While on board, or whenever a boat reached their shore, a vigorous program of trade began. [Fig. 2] Each day Midshipman John Septimus Roe entered these exchanges into the ship's log. On 25 December 1821, his concise narrative recorded: 'at 4 pm several natives on board', and at 5.10 pm 'sent the natives on shore with several presents'.[8] These meetings on board and on shore did not just involve presents being passed one way; rather they were opportunities for reciprocal exchange. Cunningham hinted at the negotiation that occurred during the transactions:

> *The natives … had been exceedingly merry on board, and thro' the medium of Biscuits our people had made some considerable Exchanges of spears, oyster crackers or stone hammers, quartz knives … throwing sticks, which they cheerfully gave up, assuring us thereby of the Confidence restored in us.*[9]

European ideas about trade were rarely just about objects, but involved arguments about morals, values and social relations.[10]

Here, Cunningham drew a connection between the willingness to trade and trust. While this trade assisted in the development of trust between the Menang and the explorers, the crew also knew they were receiving items that had been manufactured specifically for trade purposes – and they judged them accordingly. Cunningham likened the spears, hammers and knives to 'Jews' hatchets', hastily made for sale.[11] The Menang had power in these transactions too and, as the explorers' accounts suggest, the 'medium of biscuits' was set by the hosts, while the value was negotiated as part of the trade. Cunningham recorded:

> *as in civilised life [the trader] has to calculate upon the relative (and perhaps fix'd) worth of the monies of two Countries distant from each other, in his exchange of the produce of the one, for that of the other, so seems in our little commerce with these savages, when we have uniformly found it govern'd by no moderation, it was very necessary to establish a course or rate of exchange well understood by both parties.*[12]

Cunningham described the 'equitable scale of barter' as follows:

> *half a biscuit purchased a well finished barbed spear, and a like piece bought 2 or 3 knives made of fragments of quartz which are injected laterally along a stick as the handle … by the gum of the Xanthhorrea which they melt over the fire. A whole biscuit was the cost of one of their stone hammers: but 3 biscuits would … purchase one of their broad flat wammerah's [or] throwing stick, which they were very unwilling to part with owing probably to the labour and difficulty from want of proper tools in the manufacture of them.*[13]

Fig. 2   'Entrance of Oyster Harbour King George III Sound. Interview with the natives.' Sketched by
Phillip Parker King (and published by John Murray in London, May 1825); frontispiece to volume II
of King's *Narrative of a Survey of the Intertropical and Western Coasts of Australia, Performed between the
Years 1818 and 1822* (1827, first published 1826).

Courtesy British Museum

Cunningham inferred that the Menang had some control over what items were available for trade, manufacturing their hunting and fishing spears (*maungull*) for this purpose, but not their more valuable spears, which they used in warfare. The crew did not realise that the Menang had more than one type of spear. *Maungull* held less value for the Menang as such items were easier and quicker to fashion and therefore suitable for swift trade. Menang war spears – *keit* – demanded longer labour, and were a highly valuable weapon, not something to be traded away. *Keit* were longer and heavier than *maungull*, and needed to be rotated over fire until they were hard and straight. They took three or four days to make and Captain Collet Barker – the fourth commandant of the garrison – observed in 1830 that the Menang had different names for each particular part of the operation.[14]

The crew could be untrustworthy traders; Cunningham thought that 'it was soon discover'd that these poor people were easily to be outwitted, for more was to be obtained by a biscuit broken into 3 or 4 pieces than in the entire form'.[15]

News of the trade moved quickly across Menang Country, and the numbers of Aboriginal people grew each day on opposite sides of the harbour. Roe recorded in the ship's log that at 5 pm on 26 December '14 natives came on board'.[16] The following day Cunningham noted there were '17 [Menang] on the western, and 12 on the eastern side, which the novelty of (exchanging) bartering their wares for food had brought together'.[17] He believed that the Menang had arrived 'from their distant Encampment' with spears, knives of quartz, stone hammers and waddies to exchange for biscuit. However, Cunningham may have overstated the expedition's importance to the Menang; the day before, Roe recorded 'some seals playing in the water'.

13

One beached seal was killed by the Menang and the feast shared among all, providing another reason for such a large gathering. The garrison's first medical officer, Isaac Scott Nind, noted in his ethnography that the Menang dispersed into the interior in winter and 'about Christmas they commence firing the country for game, and the families who through the winter have been dispersed over the country, reassemble'.[18] Nevertheless, the trade with the voyagers was also described by Cunningham as a 'very considerable barter', and the expedition's vocabulary list, which they recorded on their third visit to King George Sound in November 1822, registered the Menang's eagerness for ship's biscuit, with the inclusion of the phrase 'To eat biscuit/Ya-mūngă-mă-ri'.[19]

Cunningham and King described the Menang as friendly and peaceful. Cunningham referred to them as 'familiar people', comparing and categorising them alongside other indigenous groups he had encountered elsewhere.[20] In tension with this friendly discourse, however, was an undercurrent of fear; these explorers expressed anxiety about their safety and security while in the company of these amicable people, always noting how close they were to the safety of their vessel, how many guns they were carrying and whether they were in range of gunfire from the brig. This fear generated further collecting; on the expedition's departure from King George Sound, the second midshipman, Frederick Bedwell took the precaution of buying all the spears on offer to avoid any violence as they set sail.[21]

As a result of their exchanges with the Menang at King George Sound, the crew of the *Bathurst* collected 'one hundred spears, thirty throwing-sticks, forty hammers, one hundred and fifty knives and a few hand-clubs'.[22] As a collector, King's instinct was to describe and categorise these items in relation to others he had either seen or collected in previous encounters around the Australian coast. King noted that the throwing sticks of the Menang 'were much more ingeniously formed than others' he had

observed elsewhere. He spent several pages in his journal detailing and sketching them. He was impressed with their portability, especially that of a spear sharpener which was fixed in a knob at the handle made from *Xanthorrhoea* gum. The sharpener was a 'small sharp-edged shell, or piece of quartz' and was used to scrape the points of spears while hunting on the move. The spears were very slender, he thought, and varied in length. They had a hole at one end so that they could be attached to the hooked point of the *meara* (spearthrower). The slender spears were cradled in the *meara* and launched with remarkable speed and accuracy. [Fig. 3] King witnessed Menang dexterity with such spears when a seal that had beached itself in the shallows of Oyster Harbour was struck by one in the neck.

Fig. 3   Spears with wooden barbs (the one on the left has a barb missing), King George Sound. The various types of wood (left to right): *Taxandria juniperina* (swamp wattle), *Eucalyptus doratoyxlon* (spearwood mallee), *Eucalyptus doratoxylon*. Probably collected December 1821 by Frederick Bedwell for Earl Mountnorris of Arley Castle, Staffordshire.

British Museum Oc 958 L 274 cm W 1.8 cm; Oc 960, L 284 cm W 2 cm; Oc. 961 L 251 cm W 1.7 cm

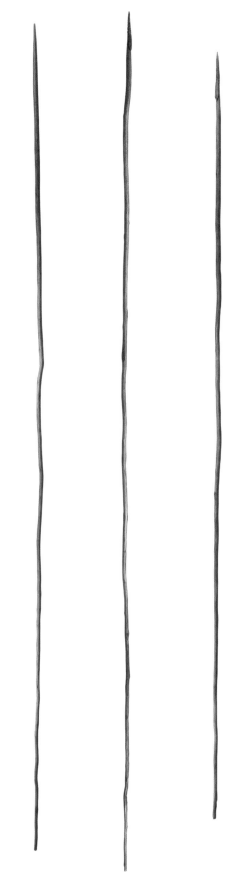

Fig. 3

Fig. 4

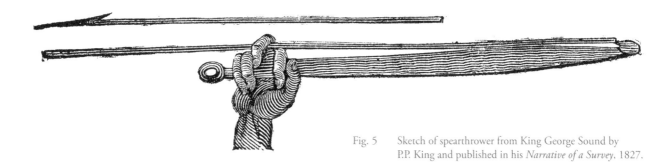

King's expedition sailed out of King George Sound on 6 January 1822. For the Menang, King's expedition was just the beginning of many years of exchange of objects for the strangers' biscuit. It was still a coveted item for the Menang when the garrison was established in December 1826. The garrison created frequent and novel opportunities for the Menang to engage in trade with newcomers. Much of this trade was mediated by Mokare, one of three brothers whose family were custodians of the Country the settlement occupied, and who befriended both Captain Collet Barker and Government Resident Alexander Collie.

In October 1830, a large group of Menang were visiting the settlement and had spent all day manufacturing *meara* and knives for the settlement's doctor, Dr Davis, in exchange for biscuit. This trade item had increased in value since King's visit in 1821. [Fig. 4, Fig. 5] Davis offered 2 lb of biscuit for each *meara* – a decent amount considering the garrison prisoners received 7 lb of biscuit in their weekly ration, and the Menang were trading *meara* and knives all day long.[23] It was not only the value which had changed, but also the construction of their tools. Captain Barker noticed:

> *Their knives [were] formerly made by fixing with the grass tree resin, sharp pieces of quartz on a piece of stick about a foot long. They now substitute for the quartz pieces of broken glass bottles, broken or sharpened so ingeniously that they can shave themselves with them.*[24]

The permanent British presence meant that ships came more frequently to Menang Country. Intense periods of trade with European visitors were possible as groups of Menang would go on board, often spending the night. To the Menang, ships – which they called *caibre* – now symbolised trade. A merchant from Hobart, William Thomas Stocker, wrote about his exchanges in 1832, when his ship *Mary Ann* anchored in the harbour. The Menang were very friendly, he recorded, and 'presented me with spears, waddies, &c., in return for which I gave them biscuit'.[25]

In the garrison, trade with soldiers was not always as intense as that which occurred on board visiting ships. Rather, it followed a more regular pace and shape. While there were times of daily bartering and manufacturing of items for trade, exchanges became incorporated into the everyday activities of the overlapping garrison and Menang worlds. The Menang received fish each time the prisoners hauled the seine and Mokare kept alert to the items upon which the soldiers put a value. He initiated a regular trade after a soldier admired one of the beautiful parrots (*towan*) that nested near the settlement in *mandianary* (November–December). They too became a currency, with the Menang travelling further to collect more *towan* for trade in the settlement when demand increased.[26]

The intense trade with King and his crew in 1821, and the trade relationships that developed in the garrison era, reveal the Menang's hospitality and openness towards visitors to their Country.

Chapter Two

'Usurping the ancient lands ...'
Mokare, Alexander Collie, and botanical collecting on Menang Country

Ian Coates and Alison Wishart

The British settlement at Albany was established on the lands of the Menang people, whose territory extended inland towards the Porongurup Range. Those Menang based at the coast often played key roles as intermediaries with the British voyagers, military personnel and later settlers. Many of the Menang artefacts now in the British Museum, and featured in this book, were collected by Dr Alexander Collie (1793–1835) in the early 1830s, most likely during his two years as Government Resident at the Albany settlement on King George Sound. [Fig. 6]

A lesser known, but no less important, legacy of Collie's time in Australia is the significant number of botanical specimens from Albany and Perth he collected and which are now held in institutions around the world. Collie sent or bequeathed over 850 specimens directly to the Royal Navy's Haslar Hospital Museum in Gosport, the Linnean Society in London and the Royal Botanic Gardens at Kew. In addition, botanist Robert Brown donated specimens Collie collected to the Natural History Museum, London, in 1857, and an auction of specimens from the Linnean Society in 1863 saw further items acquired by Kew Gardens, the Natural History Museum and possibly private collectors.[27]

The current location of this material, dispersed across institutions far from Albany, reveals something of the complex ways in which artefacts and natural history specimens were acquired and how they circulated beyond Australia during the nineteenth century. Behind both the artefacts and the botanical specimens lie relationships between Collie, Menang people – in particular, a young man called Mokare [Fig. 7] – and the landscape surrounding King George Sound.

Fig. 6   George Paul Chalmers RSA, *Portrait of Alexander Collie*, 1869, oil on panel, 28 x 23 cm.

Courtesy Chiswick Auctions

Fig. 7   Louis de Sainson (after), *Nouvelle Hollande (Port du Roi Georges)*, 1833 (published), hand-coloured lithograph, 48.7 x 32.1 cm (detail). Portrait of Mokare by de Sainson, who was the artist on the French ship *Astrolabe*.

State Art Collection, Art Gallery of Western Australia (purchased 1961)

Collie arrived on Australia's west coast in 1829 in HMS *Sulphur*, one of the first ships sent from England to establish the new Swan River Colony. Prior to this voyage, he had spent many years as both a naval surgeon and a ship's naturalist. As Daniel Simpson describes in his contribution to this volume, Collie was well connected to Scottish and English scientific networks. He saw his time in Australia as an opportunity to continue and advance these connections by collecting on behalf of the Haslar Hospital Museum: 'I am to be collector of all objects of natural history and be provided by government with the requisite articles for collecting'.[28]

For the first two years, Collie lived in Perth, during which time he accompanied various colonial officials on expeditions in the settlement's hinterland. In April 1831 he was appointed the first Government Resident at Albany and charged with overseeing its transition from a military garrison to a free settlement. There, he was able to continue his passion for natural history collecting, with a focus on botanical material. [Fig. 8] This followed his earlier botanical work in the Americas and the Pacific when he was employed as a naval surgeon in HMS *Blossom*. Collie's self-effacing nature comes through in his droll description of his botanical efforts in a letter to his brother:

> *As usual I wander a little bit into the woods and gather a few bits of flora to make me think myself a Botanist, a great naturalist, whereas others most likely set me down as a great natural.*[29]

Fig. 8   Dried specimen of *Commersonia parviflora* (Endl.), collected at Albany by Alexander Collie in the 1830s. It was later donated to the British Museum and is now the Australian National Herbarium in Canberra.

Courtesy Australian National Herbarium, Centre for Australian National Biodiversity Research, Canberra

In Western Australia's southwest, Collie was continuing the work of earlier botanical collectors who had visited the region. From 1791 to the mid-1800s, King George Sound was the focus for a series of botanists keen to collect specimens of the flora that so intrigued them, or was new to them, or was full of fascination for them. These included Archibald Menzies (1791), Robert Brown (1801) [Fig. 9] who was with Matthew Flinders, Allan Cunningham (1819–22) who accompanied Phillip Parker King, and William Baxter (1828–29). Their work laid the foundation for future collectors, including Karl Baron von Hügel (1833), Charles Darwin (1836), John Gilbert (1840), James Drummond (1840–41), Ludwig Preiss (1840–41) and John Septimus Roe (1849). By 1836, such botanical specimens had become a global commodity, with Perth-based collector James Drummond noting:

> Our flora here is of the most varied and beautiful description, the plants at King George's Sound being almost all different from those at Swan River. Persons requiring specimens of plants would be required to send paper to pack and dry them in, at least until we get a sufficient supply of that article from London.[30]

At the time of Captain George Vancouver's visit in 1791, about 250 Menang lived in the vicinity of King George Sound.[31] By 1831, when Collie arrived, the Menang had lived through 40 years of encounters with a succession of British and French expeditioners, sealers and whalers, military officers, convicts, colonial officials and, finally, a small number of free settlers. Until 1826 such encounters were usually temporary, with short trips ashore by the crews of visiting ships.[32] From 1826 this changed, when Major Edmund Lockyer from the 57th Regiment arrived to establish a small British military garrison of about 50 – mainly troops and convicts – on the northern shores of Princess Royal Harbour, on the Country belonging to Nakina, Mokare and their Menang kin.

Mokare was a Menang man and the brother of Nakina, the Menang leader at King George Sound. When Captain Jules Dumont d'Urville's French expedition arrived there in the Astrolabe in 1826, an officer on his ship described Mokare as being a young man who was more lively and talkative than his companions.[33] An artist on the ship, Louis Auguste de Sainson, painted portraits of Mokare and his kin.

Historians John Mulvaney and Neville Green have speculated that Mokare may also have met earlier British visitors such as King in 1821–22.[34] With the establishment of the garrison at Fredericks Town (now Albany) in 1826, Mokare began a series of associations with key colonial officials. Isaac Nind, the garrison surgeon, recorded that 'Mawcarri, a Native Black … resided with me [for] many months'.[35] A commandant of the settlement, Captain Collet Barker, developed a particularly close relationship with Mokare and became reliant on his knowledge and inter-cultural translation and negotiation skills.[36] Following Barker's departure, Mokare continued his association with other officials such as Collie, who explained in a letter: 'The person who abrogates to himself the title of King of the tribe, Nakinna by name, and his brother, Mokare, who serves more especially as interpreter, live at present with me'.[37]

Mokare's practice of residing with Collie, as he had earlier done with Nind, likely stemmed from them living on his family's land. Collie saw the Menang in the settlement as 'our hosts, as we certainly had come into their country and set ourselves down at, if not in, their homes and upon their territories'.[38] Thus, rather than Mokare residing with the settlers, the truth of the situation was that the settlers were residing with Mokare.

Collie and Mokare made at least four excursions inland together, the first just a few weeks after Collie's arrival. As with Barker beforehand, Collie's expeditions were heavily reliant on Mokare's intimate knowledge of the environment. He noted:

> *On the last material piece of good soil, Mokkare observed and pointed out to me the footsteps of horned Cattle and of a Horse … Mokkare had previously told me that two Bullocks and a Horse had been near this some months ago, seen by the Natives who informed him.*[39]

And on the following day:

> *Mokkare therefore conducted us SW for three-quarters of a mile, to a good sized and commodious well (native).*[40]

Mokare's practical knowledge of Country and neighbouring groups assisted Collie's travels and it is likely that the Menang names Collie recorded for various eucalypt trees he observed near the Kalgan River in May 1831 came from Mokare.[41] Perhaps it was through shared interest in the land, both as something to collect and something to explore, that Collie and Mokare were able to cross the cultural divide between them.

Mokare's work with Collie also continued a tradition of Menang assisting botanical collectors. In 1821 Menang man Jack, whom Phillip Parker King and his botanist Alan Cunningham noted as being 'truly remarkable', also helped with botanical collecting. He frequently accompanied Cunningham, 'not only assisting him in carrying his plants, but occasionally added to the specimens he was collecting'.[42]

Mokare's Countryman, Gyallipert, also assisted botanical collector Georgina Molloy who noted that in some Noongar areas, the practice of putting plants on graves deterred some Aboriginal people from assisting with botanical work.[43]

Mokare and Collie worked closely together for five months until Mokare died in August 1831. As part of the burial ceremony, Nakina broke Mokare's spear and laid it on the grave and placed his spearthrower upright in the ground beside it.[44] After Mokare's death Collie continued his collecting and exploration work, sometimes guided by other Menang men, such as Nakina and Manyat. It was with Mokare, however, that Collie had a special rapport.[45]

Alexander Collie's collections of both botanical material and Aboriginal objects from the Albany region in the early 1830s are significant for a number of reasons. They have not only enriched knowledge of natural science and Menang culture. They also form an important tangible legacy of the friendship between Collie and Mokare and other Menang who assisted in the making of Collie's collections. Equally, they testify to the contributions that the Menang made to a broader imperial collecting and mapping project, contributions that have not always been recognised and acknowledged in accounts of European natural history and science.[46]

Collie left Albany in March 1833, when he moved back to Perth to become Colonial Surgeon, a position to which he had long aspired. This was, however, to be a short-lived appointment: in 1835 Collie became seriously ill, probably with tuberculosis, and embarked on the long voyage home to England. He died in Albany, en route to Sydney, on 8 November 1835.

The importance to him of his brief association with Mokare becomes clear in his dying wish to be buried next to Mokare, his friend and companion.[47] Collie's friendships with the Menang, Mokare especially, had helped to shape his own outlook, to develop an understanding of the true nature of the relationship between 'native' and 'newcomer', and to imagine a different future, one which offered a far more radical resolution of what settlement entailed:

> *The colonist, in order to preserve a right understanding with the natives, in order to act to them as a man of civilisation, morality and religion, and in order to insure his own and family's tranquillity, success and safety, must constantly bear in mind the facts that it is he who is the primary intruder, that it is he who is usurping the ancient grounds, the undoubted property of the aborigines, who are entitled to every international law, to a full compensation, to entire satisfaction, for what they are so insidiously deprived of.*[48]

Chapter Three

For science, friendship or personal gain?
Alexander Collie and the origins of naval ethnography at Haslar Hospital Museum

Daniel Simpson

An axe, three knives, a spearthrower and a spearhead. The Menang objects collected by Alexander Collie at King George Sound in the early 1830s [Figs. 11–16] are few in number and unassuming in appearance, and yet few now doubt their significance. What they mean to Menang people today, I am not qualified to say. But there is little doubt that their contemporary meanings are imbricated with histories of encounter, dislocation and a radically changed way of life. We know little, in fact, about *how* these objects were collected, or in what circumstances, but we can make a plausible argument as to *when* and, more importantly, *why* Collie first acquired them and sent them to Britain. The meaning of collecting at the time, the objects' subsequent circulation within and between British museums, and the role they played in informing understandings of Aboriginal people must be properly explored if Collie and Mokare's honest and mutual understanding of cultural encounter and exchange during the British colonisation of Western Australia is to be emulated in the present.

An important starting point for understanding Alexander Collie's motivations for collecting from Menang people is that he was born in Scotland in 1793, and studied medicine at the University of Edinburgh.[49] Early-nineteenth century men of this background made peculiarly effective naturalists and collectors; the broad medical curricula within Scotland's universities at this time, a legacy of the Scottish Enlightenment, helped to fashion practical, engaged and experimental graduates, who saw little need to discriminate between studies of the human body, the human race and the natural world.[50] Scottish explorers, who were well represented in early colonial Australia, accordingly played a key role in furnishing museums with ethnographic objects, such as spears and shields, which sat in often chaotic assemblages among flora, fauna and human remains.[51]

The religious character of Collie's upbringing must also be borne in mind. In her authoritative study of Collie's life and career, the historian Gwen Chessell risks underestimating this point by suggesting that Collie was only a 'conventional' Christian with no overt belief in 'an all powerful creator'.[52] Although Collie never directly associated his career and philosophical interests with theological arguments or matters of faith, his early passion for natural history as well as his future relationship with Mokare are attributable in part to the religious environment in which he was raised.[53] A letter sent by Collie to his brother in October 1830 while at Cockburn Sound, near Perth, demonstrates that he considered his work in Australia in light of the moral principles taught by his family. 'May God Bless them and us all,' he wrote, 'and Grant that we may ever have the honest, upright and religious example which our most worthy parents set us before our eyes'.[54] A year later, at King George Sound, Collie informed his brother that he considered his relationship with Mokare as proof that:

> *there is here an excellent field for the missionary. Young boys would easily be accustomed to value the comforts of civilised life and thereby our moral and religious habits instilled into them. Even the older might, I think, be readily educated.*[55]

Collie's scientific and religious education evidently played a role in his motivations for encounter, but the objects he collected also reflected opportunism and self-interest. A self-professed 'canny scot', Collie combined light-hearted rivalry with his English neighbours in that 'unworthy land of Beef Steaks, roast beef and Porter' with a streak of ambition and nationalist pride that helped him to advance his position and career opportunities, both in England and in Australia.[56]

Collie's initially unremarkable employment as a British naval surgeon, for instance, changed dramatically after he came to the attention of a fellow doctor and Edinburgh graduate, the Scottish physician William Burnett, who was appointed to the Admiralty's Victualling Board and as Inspector of Hospitals in 1822.[57] Owing, at least in part, to Collie's habit of sending Burnett large quantities of Finnan haddock, a specialty of his family in Aberdeen, his subsequent employment by Burnett as a collector of ethnographic objects and specimens of natural history earned Collie rare and otherwise unobtainable commissions onboard some of the most prestigious maritime expeditions of the period.[58] Ultimately, Burnett's patronage led to Collie's appointment as Colonial Surgeon of the Swan River Colony in Western Australia.[59]

Some reference to Burnett, and his interest in Aboriginal Australia, is therefore necessary to understanding the history of the Menang objects held in the British Museum. A powerful Admiralty official, Burnett pioneered the development of systematic collecting by his surgeons through providing space for a naval museum and library, within which cultural objects and specimens of natural history from throughout the British Empire could be preserved and studied.[60] The Royal Navy's servicemen were among the best placed to collect material that informed new imperial knowledge, and they did so with great enthusiasm. Before Burnett, however, there had been a tendency to dismiss physical objects, which had great value as 'curiosities', once they had been discussed, illustrated and preserved in print within naval journals and other illustrated accounts of voyages of discovery.[61] The consequent loss of many early and valuable artefacts made by Aboriginal people in Australia and other indigenous cultures in the British world must have seemed readily apparent to Burnett in 1823, the year following his promotion, when the objects collected during the recently returned Australian expedition led by Phillip Parker King were dispersed widely among private individuals (see Gaye Sculthorpe's chapter in this volume). Nothing whatsoever was given to the British Museum, which complained about the fact for decades to come.[62]

The newly promoted Burnett wasted no time in creating an official infrastructure for naval knowledge. By 1827 a museum and library, alongside a planned botanic garden, had been constructed at one of the Royal Navy's best known institutions, The Royal Hospital Haslar.[63] [Fig. 10] The hospital, which educated and trained the Royal Navy's surgeons, was located in Gosport, near Portsmouth, making it ideally placed to access the collections and knowledge of returning expeditions. Amateur and entirely unofficial efforts to retain interesting and 'curious' things had in fact been made at Haslar since at least the eighteenth century; the hospital's cupboards and storerooms were stuffed with a bizarre assortment of items from decades of imperial voyaging, with Captain Cook's speaking trumpet and a four-legged duck among the prize objects.[64]

Fig. 10   Interior of the Royal Navy's Haslar Hospital Museum, Portsmouth, c. 1860.

Courtesy Haslar Heritage Group

Fig. 11   Axe, *kodj*, with handle made of *Agonis flexuosa*, peppermint, probably collected by Alexander Collie at King George Sound, 1831–33.

British Museum Oc 4768 L 28 cm W 11 cm

Fig. 11

Fig. 12   Fig. 13   Fig. 14

While by no means alone as an assortment of interesting specimens, the new museum at Haslar was unique in terms of its naval connection and accordingly its pedagogic focus; its opening coincided with the introduction of a program of lectures, which took place in the museum, led by Haslar's first librarian, lecturer and curator, the Edinburgh phrenologist James Scott.[65] Here, the navy's next generation of surgeons was educated among the material culture of indigenous peoples they were destined to meet, as well as the valuable plants and animals their predecessors had collected in newly colonised places, sometimes with the aid of indigenous guides and collectors.[66] The ethnographic objects in particular blended in novel ways with the students' medical education; by the 1850s, poisonous weapons had become the subject of detailed study, as naval surgeons struggled to identify cures to the unusual maladies caused by violent encounter with indigenous peoples.[67]

Being an acquaintance of Burnett and, perhaps more importantly, Scottish, Collie was appointed as Haslar's first official collector in 1825, in order that he might furnish the museum with interesting specimens before it opened.[68] Indeed, it was to Burnett's hospital museum that the majority of Collie's future collections, including the Menang axe, knives, spearthrower and spearhead were subsequently sent; between their collection in the 1830s and their transfer to the British Museum in 1855, when Haslar deaccessioned much of its ethnographic material, these objects sat at the heart of the British imperial project. As a collector, Collie was unusual both in terms of his dedication to scientific knowledge and for his considerable ability and interest in negotiating cross-cultural encounters. His first commission by Burnett onboard the voyage of HMS *Blossom*, which surveyed the Pacific and Bering Strait between 1825 and 1828, resulted in his collection of a large number of harpoons and other material from the Arctic peoples of North America, some of which now reside in the British Museum. While collectors such as King sought merit in new natural history discoveries, Collie wrote to various scientific elites in 1828 to express his 'general dislike to the very fashionable system of naming

[new specimens] after individual persons', and ordered that nothing he found was to be named after him.[69] A similarly modest attitude governed Collie's work for Haslar, which he evidently considered primarily a research, rather than a public, institution; his comprehensive notes from the *Blossom* expedition, which ran to eight volumes, were not to be 'exposed to the public more than is necessary for the good of the Museum'.[70]

Following his arrival in Western Australia on board HMS *Sulphur* in 1829, Collie continued to collect for reasons other than curiosity alone. He appears not to have acquired any spears which, as Shellam has noted in this volume, were normally chief among the objects exchanged and bartered for by early European visitors to King George Sound, owing to their cheapness and abundance. The axe, knives, spearthrower and spearhead Collie did collect, by contrast, suggest a more involved interest in Menang culture, and an inclination toward that which was rare; the three knives demonstrate the use of bottle-glass, quartz and resin in local systems of manufacture, as does the axe, which incorporates stone and gum; the spearhead in turn features fine fibre thread. As Ian Coates and Alison Wishart observe in the previous chapter, Collie was a competent botanist and perhaps sought to demonstrate the complexity and dynamism of Menang culture as well as their appreciation of the economic potential of local resources.[71]

Fig. 12   Knife, *taap*, with quartz flakes, handle of *Eucalyptus astringens*, brown mallet, probably collected by Collie at King George Sound, 1831–33.

British Museum Oc 4772 L 40 cm W 1.5 cm

Fig. 13   Knife, *taap*, with quartz flakes, handle of *Corymbia calophylla*, marri, collected by Collie at King George Sound, 1831–33.

British Museum Oc 4774 L 40 cm W 1.5 cm

Fig. 14   Knife, *taap*, with glass flakes, handle of *Corymbia calophylla*, marri, collected by Collie at King George Sound, 1831–33.

British Museum Oc 4771 L 39.5 cm W 2 cm

This was likely also an expression of the surgeon's intense and at times missionary interest in 'our compatriots the natives', whose welfare and medical condition were so often the subject of his letters home.[72] While in Australia, Collie continued to resist the temptation to use his privileged position and access to unique specimens as a means of advancing his reputation as a scientist. After 1831, his health deteriorated and he appeared to consider his debt to Burnett repaid: 'I certainly am happy in having a mind free from care,' he explained to his brother in 1832.[73] Though Collie had an 'abundance of time', and access to a 'few original materials too', the 'labour of collecting and assorting them and then the impracticality of putting them on paper' was now simply too much effort to be worthwhile.[74]

In summary, the Menang objects collected by Alexander Collie are among the earliest products of the increasingly sophisticated approach toward ethnographic study that emerged in the British naval establishment in the years following 1822. This was, perhaps, the first time that efforts to understand Menang and other indigenous cultures were taken seriously by Admiralty officials. Collie was a complex figure, and it is difficult to decide the extent to which his education and employment as Burnett's collector should be emphasised over his religious background and apparently sincere interest in encountering and engaging with the Menang people. In any case, the range and sophistication of the objects that the Scottish surgeon was able to procure, being far superior to those goods destined only for trade that had so often fooled earlier collectors such as King, was surely a product of the ambiguous boundaries between science, religion and the colonial project prevailing at that time. It is not known when precisely or how the Menang objects were first acquired, but accounts of Collie's collecting by others suggest strongly that such things nearly always originated as products of friendship and mutual understanding.

A typical such exchange occurred on 10 September 1829, when Collie was among a party who, having 'found five natives' near Canning River in Perth, gave a 'swan, some rings, knives, beads, &c., and received in exchange, spears and a stone hatchet, and parted very good friends'.[75]

Fig. 15   Spearthrower of *Eucalyptus marginata*, jarrah, with tooth or bone set in resin on end, collected by Collie at King George Sound, 1831–33.

British Museum Oc 4758 L 69.8 cm W 8 cm

Fig. 16   Spearhead of *Eucalyptus doratoxylon*, spearwood mallee, collected by Collie at King George Sound, 1831–33.

British Museum Oc 1980 Q.740 L 16 cm W 1.5 cm

Fig. 15

Fig. 16

Chapter Four

Taken out of Country
Menang objects in Britain

Gaye Sculthorpe

The artefacts collected by Alexander Collie were not the first Menang objects to reach Britain, nor the last. How were such objects acquired, who collected them, and why? Early Royal Navy ships were stocked with specific goods for trade with indigenous peoples. On his visit in 1791, George Vancouver deposited 'beads, nails, looking glasses, and medals' in an empty hut as 'tokens of our friendly disposition' and other goods to compensate for wood taken.[76] Men sailing with Matthew Flinders in 1801 had direct contact with Menang who found the British trade goods offered of little use and 'they made very early signs to our gentlemen to return from whence they came'.[77] Although the assistant-surgeon on Flinders' ship, Mr Purdie, exchanged some metal and 'toys' for 'some of their implements', no artefacts from these early voyages are known to have survived.[78]

By the time of Phillip Parker King's second visit in December in 1821, Menang men were experienced traders with visitors. As Tiffany Shellam has shown in her book, *Shaking Hands on the Fringe* (2009), and her contribution to this volume, Menang made strategic decisions about what objects they were willing to trade with outsiders and quickly made some items specifically for exchange purposes. During King's stay, he and his crew collected over 320 artefacts, mainly knives (*taap*) and spears, but also spearthrowers, axes (*kodj*) and a few clubs.[79] As these were collected prior to the establishment of the Royal Navy's Haslar Hospital Museum, at the end of the voyage they were dispersed widely to interested and often competing collectors in Britain such as George Annesley, the 2nd Earl Mountnorris (1770–1844).

Styled Viscount Valentia until the death of his father in 1816, Annesley was born and raised at Arley Castle in Staffordshire. Educated at Rugby School and Oxford University, he was a member of the Royal Society, a Fellow of the Linnean Society and the Literary Society of London. An avid collector of books, antiquities, art, and natural history, in 1815 he published *Short Instructions for Collecting Shells*. Although he asked the Reverend Ralph Mansfield in Sydney to make a collection of natural history for him in 1834, his Australian collecting appears to have started more than a decade earlier.[80]

Frederick Bedwell (1776–1853), along with John Septimus Roe (1797–1878), was a midshipman with King on the *Mermaid*, and the *Bathurst*. Bedwell had entered the Royal Navy in 1810 as a nominee of Valentia, who was his godfather.[81] Daniel Simpson's recent research has uncovered specific links between Bedwell and Mountnorris' collecting. In 1821 and 1823, Mountnorris wrote of his 'New Holland collections' and his young protégé, a lieutenant of the Royal Navy, who was surveying Australia.[82] Their closeness is also evident in Bedwell's later naming his home near Paterson in New South Wales 'Valentia'. The Australian objects in Mountnorris' collection all come from places associated with Bedwell: Hanover Bay and King George Sound in Western Australia; Port Jackson and Clarence River in New South Wales; and Lizard Island in Queensland. Throughout King's voyage Bedwell was often collecting artefacts, and sometimes plants, when he went on shore.

Fig. 17   Arley Castle in Staffordshire, home of Earl Mountnorris, c. 1852.
Frederick Bedwell collected Menang and other Aboriginal objects for him.

Courtesy British Museum

At King George Sound on 29 December 1821 extensive bartering occurred. The Aboriginal man King called 'Jack' formed a close relationship with the visitors, who noted: 'he was the only native who did not manufacture spears for barter, for he was evidently convinced of the superiority of our weapons and laughed heartily whenever a bad and carelessly-made spear was offered to us for sale'. The next day, as the boat was about to leave, Menang people came again to barter spears, throwing-sticks and knives. Bedwell 'purchased all the spears the natives had brought down, that, in case they should feel angry at his leaving them, they might have no weapons to do any mischief with … While Mr. Bedwell was purchasing the spears and other weapons Jack brought him a throwing-stick that he had previously concealed behind a bush and sold it to him for a biscuit'.[83] Bedwell returned to the UK after this voyage, but in 1827 he came back to live in Australia.

Although Mountnorris wished his extensive collection to be kept together after his death, it was auctioned at an 11-day sale at Arley Castle in 1852. [Fig. 17] The ethnographic objects were displayed 'on the staircase' and sold on the second day of the sale. Quaker collector Henry Christy acquired these and other objects which subsequently came to the British Museum as part of the Christy Collection. The three King George Sound spears and spearthrower ('throwing stick') from Arley Castle thus represent not only the earliest surviving organic items of Menang material heritage but also some of the oldest such objects ever collected in Australia.

Collie was the major collector of early Menang objects in the 1830s. As he lived at Albany from early 1831 until 1833, and then just briefly before he died there in 1835, it can be assumed the artefacts he collected date from this period. Unlike the very long spears from the collection of Mountnorris, the axes and knives collected by Collie are small and would have been far easier to pack and transport to Haslar Hospital Museum. Some of these objects are marked specifically 'King George's Sound' and labelled with the word 'Collie' (or 'Collier'). There are other similar objects, which came to the British Museum in 1855 from Haslar, that have registration numbers in sequence with these, suggesting that they may also have come from Collie, but no catalogue of the Haslar Hospital Museum has yet been found.

After Collie's death, in line with his will, his natural history collections were sent to various scientific institutions in the UK. This included a tin box addressed to Sir William Burnett, who played a key role in establishing the museum at Haslar.[84] It is likely that this case included Collie's objects that were later donated by the Admiralty to the British Museum. By sending them back to Haslar, Collie was depositing them in a museum for posterity and for the future dissemination of knowledge.

From 1852, steamships began to call regularly at Albany, which was strategically positioned on the important shipping route to the east coast of Australia and to New Zealand. A number of their passengers showed an interest in Menang culture and collected objects, most only an item or two. Little is known about the circumstances of collection, but it is known that several of these men were sympathetic observers of Maori life in New Zealand.

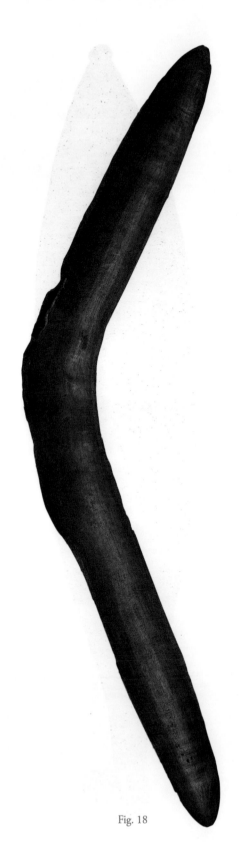

Fig. 18

One such passenger was Frederick Meinertzhagen (1845–1895). In 1866, he had emigrated from London to New Zealand and became a sheep breeder and an active collector of Maori artefacts. In 1870–71, he returned to Britain for a period and visited the privately owned Christy Collection as well as the British Museum to view the Maori collections. As the boomerang from his collection is labelled 'King George's Sound 1870', it can be assumed that it was acquired there during transit on his way to London. [Fig. 18] In 1881 Meinertzhagen and his family returned permanently to the UK, where his wife, two daughters and an adopted Maori son died of scarlet fever shortly after their arrival. On Meinertzhagen's own death in 1895, his daughter Gertrude donated his extensive Maori collection, along with this boomerang, several knives and a shield to the British Museum.[85]

In 1864, English cricketer Edward Mills Grace, brother of W.G. Grace, had a brief stop at Albany on his way home after a tour of Australia. During an excursion on land, he gathered some flowers and was 'immensely bothered' by Menang seeking sixpences and shillings. He purchased a boomerang for a shilling and competed in an impromptu 100-yard race with an Aboriginal man.[86] Henry Littleton (1844–1933) was another passing passenger. An Englishman, son of Baron Hatherton, Littleton arrived in Australia in 1866 and bought property in Queensland. He worked as a private secretary for both Governor Sir George Bowen of Victoria and Sir Hercules Robinson, Governor of New South Wales. Littleton acquired Aboriginal artefacts from central Queensland through a man named Gilbert, who was an Inspector of Native Police in the Gilbert Ranges in the 1870s.

Fig. 18   Boomerang *Allocasuarina fraseriana*, sheaok, collected by Frederick Meinertzhagen, King George Sound, 1870.

British Museum Oc 1895,-.467 L 53.5 cm W 5.5 cm

Of the 16 Aboriginal objects Littleton donated to the British Museum, only one, a spearthrower, is from King George Sound. It is likely he collected it while transiting at Albany on the P&O ship *Assam* in 1879, the year he returned to live in England.[87] [Fig. 19]

The Reverend Alfred Watson Hands (1849–1927) also visited Albany on his way back Britain in 1887 to retire after seven years in New Zealand. Like Meinertzhagen, Hands had an interest in Maori people and knowledge. Born in London, he was a man of many talents: an architect, minister, amateur artist, botanist and natural historian. His many watercolour sketches, now held in New Zealand institutions, include a detailed drawing of insects and plants with Maori names written beside each.[88] When the SS *Carthage* stopped at Albany in February 1887, Hands collected a seed (possibly a gum nut) which he later sketched on board ship, as well as a spearthrower, now in the Pitt Rivers Museum in Oxford.

He also made a watercolour sketch of an Aboriginal family at Albany. [Fig. 20] Painted against a backdrop of hills, it sympathetically portrays the group wearing blankets. He may have met these individuals during his short excursion on land. Although there are early engravings depicting Menang in the 1820s, such drawings of Menang people from the late 1800s are rare.

Fig. 19

Fig. 19   Spearthrower of *Eucalyptus marginata*, jarrah, collected by Henry Littleton, King George Sound, 1870.

British Museum Oc 1929, 0114.6 L 57 cm W 12.5 cm

Fig. 20   *Natives of Western Australia*, watercolour sketch
by Rev. Alfred Watson Hands, Albany, 1887.

Pitt Rivers Museum 1934.79.7 H 26.4 cm W 18.2 cm

One Albany resident, Henry Toll (1827–1907), was a
small collector of Menang objects. Born in Devon, Toll
emigrated to Albany in November 1863 and spent about
12 years living in that region.[89] He held a number of
positions including working for the P&O Company, and
serving as a member of the town council, vice-president
of the Mechanics Institute, Consul for the United States
of America, and chairman of the Education Board. After
receiving a gratuity from the P&O Company, he became
a squatter near the Stirling Range in the Porongurup area
but this sheep farming venture failed.[90] In the 1880s, he
served for at time as lighthouse keeper on Breaksea Island.
He returned to live in Britain. In 1905, the year before his
death, he made a visit back to Albany to see his children.

It is likely that the objects he collected were acquired
during his time in the Porongurup area as a letter to the
Western Daily Mercury in Plymouth in 1898 notes:

> *I have passed 12 years of my life in the wilds of
> Western Australia, and in connection with the
> above facts, I propose next week to present to the
> Municipal Museum at Beaumont Park some
> weapons used by these aboriginal blacks in their
> native tribal wars. As there is now in Plymouth
> a safe place of deposit for these antiquated curios,
> I further purpose sending a notched stick, which,
> in the native pigeon-English they term 'paper
> talk', and was sent me by an athletic tribal
> chief who lorded it over the Toolbrunup Hills,
> forming part of the Stirling Ranges. The message
> conveyed by notches on this stick was 'Loving
> Greeting' with an invite to my wife and self 'to
> come back again and rejoin them in their own
> mountain home'.*[91]

Unfortunately, several of the items Toll donated to the
Plymouth Museum in 1898, just after it opened, were
stolen in 1901–02, including the message stick referred to
above. Yet the museum retains several others including two
spearthrowers and a knife. These varied examples show that
Menang objects were collected in the 1800s as objects for
rich patrons such as Mountnorris, for future learning as
with Collie, and as mementoes of travellers and residents
who took an interest in other cultures. Later visitors could
purchase images of Menang on postcards to send back
home [Fig. 21] The changing circumstances of Menang
meant that most of their own object types were replaced by
European goods for daily use. The need for a local museum
in Albany was discussed in the 1890s yet it would take
many decades for Menang history and culture to feature in
public institutions locally. The Menang objects in museums
in Britain thus constitute a major record of early Menang
material culture, and the exhibition of some of these
objects in Albany in 2016 is highly significant.

Fig. 21   *Native Women at Albany.* Postcard printed for Todd's Book Arcade, Albany, probably
early 1900s. The handwritten message on the front reads: 'Western Australia.
Landed here + stayed two days'.

British Museum Oc B141.11 H 8.8 cm W 14 cm

Chapter Five

Menang and European relations at nineteenth-century Albany

Murray Arnold

The story of Aboriginal–European relations at Albany and its surrounding region during the early decades following permanent British settlement represents an exception to the almost universal Australian experience. In late December 1826, the *Amity* sailed into Princess Royal Harbour on an expedition intended to plant the British flag in the west. Major Edmund Lockyer and the rest of those on board, and the local Menang people who witnessed the ship's arrival, chose a path characterised by a degree of tolerance and cooperation that was in marked contrast to the hostility and bloodshed which commonly existed on the frontiers of settlement. However, the relationship was never idyllic. Once the Menang realised that those who had set up camp in their midst had no intention of leaving, and were in fact openly claiming ownership over the land which had provided their material and spiritual nourishment for tens of thousands of years, some disharmony became inevitable. [Fig. 22]

There are several reasons why this period of Albany's history proved atypical. First, Major Lockyer and his 20 soldiers, 23 convicts, surgeon, gardener, and storekeeper, together with three soldiers' wives and two of their children, had not come with the usual intention of establishing a settlement of free British men and women bent on turning the bush into farmland. Rather they were there because of a justifiable fear on the part of the British Colonial Office that the French government had designs on the western side of a continent that both nations saw as essentially empty land.[92] [Fig. 23] The Port Macquarie penal settlement had proved unsatisfactory, and a replacement needed to be found.[93] Perhaps planting the Union Jack at King George Sound would serve this purpose, and forestall possible French ambitions in the enormous region west of the existing colonies in eastern Australia. Although the British were expected to grow their own vegetables, net fish and raise small numbers of livestock for food, there were no plans to extend the footprint of settlement beyond a few acres near the harbour shore.

Second, the small number of British at Albany meant that Aboriginal food sources were not put under increased pressure. It is actually probable that the Menang people's diet was enhanced by their association with the newcomers, who shared the plentiful fish netted in the harbour and quickly taught local men how to use muskets to hunt kangaroos and birds.

Third, the friendly and curious nature of several of the most influential people from each group was another factor that led to the early formation of a harmonious relationship. Those in charge of the garrison made sure that friendly relations were maintained wherever possible, beginning with Lockyer's refusal to retaliate when a young convict was almost fatally speared soon after the *Amity* arrived and carrying through to the practice of each of his three successors.

Fig. 23   Louis de Sainson; Langume and Leborne, *Aiguade de l'Astrolabe au Port du Roi Georges (N'elle Hollande)*, 1826 (painted), 1833 (published), coloured lithograph, 28.6 x 38.5 cm. Artists on French voyages, such as de Sainson, made important visual records of Menang and their encounters with Europeans.

State Art Collection, Art Gallery of Western Australia (purchased 1955)

Certainly, the British were well aware of their precarious position in the event of a serious Aboriginal attack, but their actions in befriending several Menang men and scrupulously behaving in a positive manner towards all of the Aboriginal people who frequented the settlement, whether on a regular or a casual basis, show that fear was not their only motive. Similarly, Mokare and his brothers, on whose land the tiny settlement existed, chose to coexist peacefully in a close relationship with the British, rather than, for instance, either ignoring their presence or mounting an armed attack.

Effectively, the British became permanent, if uninvited, guests on Menang land for the four years that the garrison existed, and the behaviour of both groups during that period indicates that each saw the relationship at least partly in those terms. The fourth commandant, Captain Collet Barker, kept a comprehensive daily journal during his 15-month stay at Albany; in particular, it detailed his extraordinary friendship with Mokare.

The young man frequently slept on the floor of Barker's small hut, and the two spent many evenings around the fire enquiring into the finer points of each other's culture. Their friendship grew out of mutual respect, and this carried over into the overall relationship between the two very different groups who had been thrown together by the decision to establish a British presence at King George Sound.

The decision to incorporate the settlement into the newly proclaimed colony of Western Australia in March 1831 profoundly altered the purpose and future of European settlement at Albany.[94] For the first time, the town and region became available for free settlers to gain exclusive title to land and to use it to further their own economic ends. Those living there when the change was announced fully appreciated that as a result the relationship with the Menang would come under severe pressure.

Barker wrote in his journal regarding a discussion he had with Mokare about the future:

> Mokare said several were now talking of settling with the whites, but they must have shirt & trowsers, or they would be obliged to go the bush to spear Kangaroo … Mokare again told me again in the evening that they talked of coming to stop constantly about King Geo[rge Sound] … On Asking M if his people would make good shepherds … he said 'yes', that just at first they might not but in a little time.[95]

Fortunately, the first Government Resident, Alexander Collie, realised the importance of maintaining good relations and became a close friend of Mokare. In June 1831 Mokare went into the bush, but returned to the settlement, critically ill, late the following month. Collie took him into his home and nursed him until his death in the first week of August. He took great care to ensure that his friend was buried according to Menang tradition, and later even requested that he be buried alongside Mokare. This wish was complied with on Collie's death in 1835, but in 1840 his body was moved to the newly established Albany cemetery, while Mokare still lies in an unmarked grave at the original site somewhere behind Albany's Town Hall.

The anticipated rush of free settlers failed to materialise. The natural level of soil fertility in the Albany region was so abysmally low that nineteenth-century technology proved utterly incapable of delivering profitable yields of broad-acre cereal crops, or even good pasture suitable for livestock grazing on a large scale.

Many potential settlers came to Albany seeking to take up land for farming purposes, but the overwhelming majority immediately left for more promising districts. Only a very few found small pockets of soil suitable for farming. It would be more than a hundred years before the availability of suitable fertilisers and trace elements allowed wide-scale land clearing to take place within a radius of 100 kilometres of the town.

This proved very fortunate for the subsequent history of Aboriginal–European relations in the region, since it meant that the Menang were able to continue for decades to live on their traditional land and practise their culture in ways that their compatriots in the more intensively settled areas found difficult or impossible to emulate. As late as 1881, census figures show that the town of Albany had a European population of only 1,024, with just 691 settlers occupying an area of 20 million acres to its north. Fifty years after this vast region was made available for farming, only 886 acres of bushland had been cleared.[96] Much of the remaining area was used from the 1840s by pastoralists who ran cattle and sheep in the uncleared bush under licences specifically permitting Aboriginal people continued access to the land.

Following the commencement of free settlement, some Menang people chose to live in the town of Albany, taking employment as labourers or domestic servants, or as crew members on the small vessels engaged in whaling ventures close to the town. Others remained inland and seldom or never interacted in any way with the British. All were adversely affected in the early 1840s by the arrival of significant numbers of people from two very different groups not closely connected to either the Menang or the original British settlers. The entire social fabric of the town was exposed to the socially and culturally corrosive influence of large numbers of crew members from ships arriving at the port. Between April 1840 and March 1841, 25 American and three French whaling vessels, together with a further 19 ships, called in for supplies and repairs.

As many as 300 men were in Albany at a time, all more or less under the influence of alcohol, and the small number of local police proved totally unable to maintain control.[97] Some of these seamen provided spirits to Aboriginal people, with the result that the relatively harmonious relationship built up since 1826 began to break down.

At the same time, Aboriginal people from other groups well to the east of Albany began to participate in the bi-monthly distribution of flour authorised by the town's Resident Magistrate as rations in reward for the Menang people's cooperative behaviour. This proved culturally disruptive, and led to a worsening of relations with settlers since the Aboriginal visitors from the east were not so inclined to respect British concepts of land ownership and private property – two fundamental pillars of that society. The very few farmers who lived in Albany's hinterland found themselves in a precarious position as Aboriginal people began to take their produce and spear their animals. For the first time, violent conflict threatened to erupt in the region following an altercation at Hassell's Kendenup property approximately 80 kilometres north of Albany. One of a party of 40 men from the eastern group fatally speared a European station employee during a regular flour distribution. In response, these distributions were discontinued, with the result that the eastern Aboriginal visitors ceased their travels to Menang land and relations returned to their former state.[98]

In 1860, a tragic event occurred which profoundly affected the Menang people. The *Salsette* entered the port of Albany with measles on board, and the disease quickly spread throughout the town and region, eventually reaching York and Perth. Aboriginal people had no natural immunity to protect them and died in large numbers. Arthur Trimmer, in his capacity of Sub-guardian of Natives at Albany wrote to Perth stating: 'every native [in Albany] to the amount of sixty-four has suffered, and out of that number twenty-nine have died'.[99]

Two weeks later, Trimmer reported the deaths of a further 200 from the surrounding areas, a mortality rate he estimated at 50 per cent. From this time until the mid-twentieth century very few Aboriginal people lived in the town of Albany, choosing instead to move inland to areas to the north. There they were able to maintain much of their traditional way of life while coming under increasing influence from the small but growing numbers of Europeans making their living as pastoral workers, sandal-wood cutters or kangaroo shooters.

The 1854 census reveals a striking fact – while there were 165 free men living in either Albany or its hinterland, there were another 348 in the same area who had been transported to the colony as convicts. Most of these were living isolated lives working as shepherds or in other forms of employment that put them into close, and frequently socially destructive, contact with Aboriginal people. Only nine single European women then lived in the town and surrounding region and many liaisons between Aboriginal women and convict men, including marriage, developed as a result.

This extended period, during which European numbers in the region were quite low, eventually came to an end when the Great Southern Rail line between Beverley and Albany opened in mid-1889. The settler population increased significantly as farmers cleared and fenced the more fertile areas that the new line opened up well to Albany's north, and the relationship between Aboriginal people and Europeans quickly began to change. Aboriginal people increasingly saw their spiritually significant sites damaged, while their sources of water were commandeered for livestock and household use. Seeking casual employment as farm workers, many moved into the new towns and rail sidings while successfully retaining to this day much of the Menang tradition and culture handed down from their forefathers.

I was privileged to attend the viewing of our local Menang artifacts that had returned from the British Museum and displayed in the National Museum in Canberra.

I examined each item closely and could envisage my forefathers shaping each one, when the artifacts come to Albany it will be a showcase for all Australia.

Averil Dean, Menang Elder, 2016

Fig. 23   Robert Havell and Robert Dale, *Panoramic view of King George's Sound,*
part of the colony of Swan River, 1834, hand-coloured aquatint, 19 x 274.2 cm.

Courtesy National Library of Australia 139546509

...hart of the colony of Swan River.

Panoramic view of King George

Chapter Six

The Keepers

Harley Coyne and John Carty

In 2015 and 2015–16 respectively, the British Museum and the National Museum of Australia hosted major exhibitions of Aboriginal and Torres Strait Islander culture and history. Much has been written and debated publicly about these exhibitions – *Indigenous Australia: Enduring Civilisation* and *Encounters: Revealing Stories of Aboriginal and Torres Strait Islander Objects from the British Museum* – but the making of them was a process far more transformative for each museum than any exhibition could tell. The story behind that process played out in communities around Australia, as the two museums consulted with them about the most meaningful objects to be exhibited, and even the most meaningful *places* for them to be exhibited.

From 2011 to 2015 the British Museum and the National Museum of Australia partnered with the Australian National University to lay open this process of making the exhibitions – one in London, the other in Canberra – and to invite scholarly, critical and cultural feedback on the processes of consultation. This project – entitled *Engaging Objects: Indigenous Communities, Museum Collections and the Representation of Indigenous Histories* – examined how the British Museum's Indigenous Australian collections were being activated, and their history and meaning interpreted and challenged, through the processes of community engagement.[100]

The British Museum is obviously a complex site of symbolic (and often material) contestation in Australia. The display of its Aboriginal and Torres Strait Islander collections, whether in Britain or Australia, is laden with the tensions of ongoing and unsettled histories. The process of consultation with Australian communities has opened up new dialogues with museums, but also new dialogues *about* museums. Throughout the community consultations, Aboriginal concepts of heritage, of materiality, of history, of Country provided ongoing challenges to the status and interpretation of specific objects but also to the ongoing role of the museum in relationship to them.

During this process of consultation, the most concrete challenge of all came from Menang Country:

> You can take those artefacts to Canberra, we're not going to stop you. But we're telling you something else is possible here. We're saying there's something more meaningful you could do … if you're serious.
>
> Harley Coyne, 2012

I feel a sense of ownership in bringing these objects home.

Lindsay Dean, Emerging Curator, Menang, 2016

Harley Coyne

I have always had an interest in museums and keeping places and this has grown on a number of fronts more recently. I currently work for a government department, and one of our programs is to facilitate the repatriation of more than 400 sets of Aboriginal Ancestral remains back into Country across Western Australia. The remains are kept in the Western Australian Museum and along with other regional heritage officers we work with Aboriginal communities, local government and others to put our Ancestors back into Country.

Ancestral remains are regularly exposed through natural processes or development activity, while others have been unearthed as part of studies undertaken by archaeologists and anthropologists. Having been involved directly in the successful repatriation of over 50 sets of Ancestral remains across my Country has been one of the most satisfying experiences I have had in life so far. I have shared this experience with my youngest son by having him present and involved in burial ceremonies which for both of us has been quite an experience. The numbers of our Ancestors currently held in the Western Australian Museum is down to about 100 as a result of this program. The repatriation program is often very challenging and it regularly tests your resolve both morally and culturally, but it is incredibly rewarding for all involved. It was against this backdrop, and these ongoing responsibilities, that I became involved in these broader questions of returning objects with museums.

In 2012 we, as members of the Noongar and Menang community, met with representatives from the National Museum of Australia who were in Albany to discuss a proposed exhibition in London and Canberra of about 150 objects from the British Museum. These historic artefacts had been collected from Aboriginal and Torres Strait Islander communities across Australia. The British Museum sought our approval to exhibit four items from its collection from the Albany region in the 1830s in an exhibition planned for 2015.

Images of the artefacts were presented to the community and their origins discussed. We were impressed by the fact that the objects had been so well preserved and that they came from the period of initial contact around the 1830s. Many of these items were collected by people who came to our Country as government representatives from England or Scotland as part of the settlement of this continent. Much detail has been recorded about how the items were collected and traded for goods and services (see the other chapters in this volume). Alexander Collie and his noted close relationship with Mokare is confirmed not only by Collie's desire to be buried side by side with his friend, but also by our understanding that some items were exchanged as part of their early encounters.

Fig. 24   Harley Coyne shows Ian Coates (National Museum of Australia) and John Carty
(South Australia Museum) around the cultural landscapes of Menang Country, 2012.

Courtesy Benita Tunks

The discussions with our community were double-edged: filled with optimism about the return to Australia of the objects, but also disappointment at the fact that we might not get to see them back in our Country. Questions were raised about who we were talking to in the first instance, as the people visiting us were representatives from the National Museum of Australia and not those from the British Museum, who we thought should be present. What would be gained for our community by giving approval to an exhibition of our artefacts in a place nearly 3,000 kilometres away and in three years' time?

We asked if the artefacts could be brought to Albany and shown to our people on their arrival in Australia prior to the exhibition in Canberra, or alternatively on their way back to London. This proposition was unsuccessful in the first instance. Questions about the ownership of the artefacts also came out of the discussions.

Serious concerns were raised about the length of time it was going to take for the return of the objects and if we were going to be able to share this experience with some of our elders. We regularly lose elders from our community to old age and other afflictions and the proposed exhibition at that point was three years away. There is an urgency to these questions in communities around the country. In this case the exhibition in Canberra did not have the same value for us that it had for the two museums.

We had reservations about the processes with more questions than answers. Interviews were conducted with many people who expressed diverse views about the objects:

> *You've got the sticks and that but we've got the stories and without the stories the sticks mean nothing. They need to come back here so that we could put these stories to them and they could be told in a way that our ancestors would want them told.*

> *Treasy Woods, 2012*

What was clear, however, was the dissatisfaction people felt at only talking to the National Museum of Australia curators – we wanted to be addressed directly by the museum that was holding our cultural materials, the British Museum. However, we did have some resolution as its representatives visited our community shortly after the initial meetings and ongoing discussions with them were fruitful. This we felt was an appropriate response. We agreed to have our artefacts shown in the *Encounters: Revealing Stories of Aboriginal and Torres Strait Islander Objects from the British Museum* exhibition at the National Museum of Australia in 2015 because they would be part of some of the oldest and rarest Aboriginal and Torres Strait Islander artefacts shown in this significant event.

More than 98,000 people saw that show in Canberra and it clearly had a big impact. But our initial concerns still held. Of those 98,000 people, only two Noongar elders from our community were able to attend. That exhibition had great value, but it was not the value we were asking the museums to work towards locally.

From the beginning our community asked for our artefacts to come back to Country and in recognition of this the British Museum resolved to try to make this happen. The Western Australian Museum has a branch in Albany and it is also accredited as an exhibiting museum under the *Protection of Objects on Loan Act 2013*. This allowed the parties to coordinate a local exhibition of artefacts home here in Menang Country from November 2016 until April 2017. The *Yurlmun: Mokare Mia Boodja* exhibition – the title means 'Returning to Mokare's Home Country' – was the result of this resolve.

The exhibition provided us with the opportunity to see, firsthand, the artefacts that were collected here over 180 years ago. A reconnection ceremony was organised for members of the community giving them the opportunity to sit with and be with the artefacts through a private viewing. Our community looked forward to the physical and the spiritual connections that are manifest in these objects. Elders expressed their anticipation at having a first-hand look at the ways in which these items were manufactured and the materials used. At our request, scientists at the British Museum conducted scientific tests on the wood used in manufacturing the objects so that we could have a contemporary view of their origins. The community organised a number of events in support of the exhibition so that the experience and history of these items could be shared with the wider community.

I currently sit on a Peoples Panel for the development of Western Australia's $420 million New Museum, which is one of the most significant museum developments in the world today. When it is completed in 2020, the New Museum will provide an opportunity to reflect on the diversity of Aboriginal culture and heritage throughout the facility as a cornerstone in its design and programs. Together with the museum, we will promote Aboriginal heritage and culture and ensure it can be better understood and acknowledged as an essential part of Australian society.

Museums and other institutions have an obligation to be more accountable to Aboriginal communities because collections of currently held Ancestral remains, artefacts, paintings and information from our communities must be shared and our authority in managing these things should be recognised and acknowledged. For museums to have any true legitimacy in today's society, then, they need to change and incorporate Aboriginal perspectives into their policies. It is a cultural and moral obligation.

I see change in the way Aboriginal people have been treated and have experienced it in many ways having been born prior to the 1967 referendum which recognised that we did exist and needed to be included in Australian society. There are many things that still need to be resolved, including constitutional recognition for Aboriginal and Torres Strait Islander people, a treaty and improved outcomes in relation to health, education and a raft of other issues. We have had some losses along the way, but the gains made will be celebrated.

Bringing objects from London back to Canberra is for the majority of Aboriginal people who live in Albany, and never go to Canberra, not a high priority. People understand the value of such an endeavour. But it isn't their game, and it usually isn't what they wanted to focus on.

What people around Australia asked for is for the museum to bring itself to them. Museums call it outreach, or community engagement, or whatever. But it's more than that: there is a conceptual and political challenge here in this growing imperative for the decentering of museums, in this demand for museums to be unhinged from the bricks and mortar model. Museums in Australia, if they are to evolve into relevant institutions in dialogue with Aboriginal people, need to find new ways of expressing a commitment to shared values. The desire for objects to return to Country addresses a range of cultural, emotional, political and historical issues. It also cuts to the heart of the changing logic of museums.

Country itself is about our deepest context. Its centrality to the meanings and politics of Aboriginal peoples and cultures in Australia challenges some of the core premises and practices – of taking objects out of their original context – upon which museums are built. We believe that this offers an evolutionary impetus to the ways in which we continue to rethink the 'museum'. Unhooking museums from their physical locations, and releasing objects back into the flow of culture and contemporary life is one way forward.

Museums, as agents in and receptacles of colonial processes, are often pitted against Indigenous values and concepts of heritage. There are, in the historical emergence of the modern museum, obvious and well-founded reasons for these tensions. But, as we have found over the last few years, these are neither fixed nor insurmountable positions. Museums are growing up, and that will involve changing attitudes, behaviours and values. It will involve more conversations and more listening. But it is happening.

There are more complex and less oppositional frameworks built on genuine dialogue that have been emerging during the consultations around the British Museum objects over the last few years. We hope that the return of objects to Menang Country will act as a model to help museums and communities to find new ways forward and to challenge each other to find new understandings of our shared history leading into a joint custodianship of the future.

In the same way that the positive relationship between Collie and Mokare saw these objects collected, the relationship between Menang community and the British Museum, the National Museum of Australia and partners has seen them brought back to Country.

Fig. 26   Lynette Knapp explaining things to Lissant Bolton (British Museum) and Ian Coates (National Museum of Australia), 2012.

Courtesy John Carty

A note on wood species

Caroline Cartwright

The objects from the British Museum's collections from King George Sound and Albany were examined in the British Museum's Department of Scientific Research in July 2016. In each case, the wood species is identified on the relevant caption in this publication.

Tiny samples of wood were taken from each artefact for wood species identification. Sampling was carried out in already-damaged or unobtrusive areas that did not have decoration, pigments, insect damage or adhesive, so that the fine details of the cellular structure were visible for study. Following standards of the International Association of Wood Anatomists, each wood sample was sub-divided into transverse, radial longitudinal and tangential longitudinal sections in order to microscopically examine all the anatomical features.[101]

Each sub-divided wood sample was then placed uncoated on an adhesive carbon disc mounted onto an aluminium stub; no other sample preparation was required. Examination of the mounted wood samples and comparative reference specimens of wood from Western Australia was undertaken at very high magnifications in the Hitachi S-3700N variable pressure scanning electron microscope (SEM) so that the characteristic cellular structure and other diagnostic features could be identified.

The SEM gives much higher magnifications, resolution and detail than can be achieved with an optical microscope. As the samples were in different conditions of preservation, a small amount of air was allowed into the chamber of this specialised variable pressure type of SEM to get the best results.

The analytical detector attached to the SEM was used to provide elemental identification where necessary; for example, to see whether crystals and inclusions in the wood cells were calcium or silica. This information indicates the types of soils in which the trees were growing.

Few historical observers at King George Sound recorded the species of wood used to make artefacts. Phillip Parker King noted in 1821 that spears were made from 'a species of leptospermum that grows abundantly in swampy places'. The identification of wood from the artefacts in the British Museum show that spears used in this region were made also from spearwood mallee (*Eucalyptus doratoxylon*) and swamp wattle (*Taxandria juniperina*); spearthrowers from jarrah (*Eucalyptus marginata*); knife handles from marri (*Corymbia calophylla*) and brown mallet (*Eucalyptus astringens*); axe handles were of swamp wattle and peppermint (*Agonis flexuosa*), and boomerangs of she-oak (*Allocasuarina fraseriana*).

The southwest region of Australia has a high degree of biodiversity. While historical records indicate evidence of large-scale communal gatherings and trade and exchange, these objects are all made of wood species that can be found within the southwest region. This research also shows the extent to which different wood properties, such as grain, strength, durability and workability, were understood and sought out by the Aboriginal makers of these objects.

Fig. 27   Axe, *kodj*, with handle made of *Taxandria juniperina*, swamp wattle, collected at King George Sound, c. 1855–70.

British Museum Oc 4769 L 28 cm

Fig. 27

Further reading

Arnold, M., *A Journey Travelled: Aboriginal-European Relations at Albany and the Surrounding Regions from First Contact to 1926*. UWA Publishing, Crawley, Western Australia, 2015.

Chessell, G., *Alexander Collie: Colonial Surgeon, Naturalist and Explorer*, UWA Press, Crawley, Western Australia, 2008.

Clarke, P.A., *Aboriginal Plant Collectors: Botanists and Australian Aboriginal People in the Nineteenth Century*, Rosenberg Publishing, Kenthurst, New South Wales, 2008.

King, P.P., *Narrative of a Survey of the Intertropical and Western Coasts of Australia, Performed between the Years 1818 and 1822*, vol. 1 and 2, John Murray, London, 1827.

Konishi, S., M. Nugent and T. Shellam (eds), *Indigenous Intermediaries: New Perspectives on Exploration Archives*, ANU Press, Canberra, 2015.

Mulvaney, J. and N. Green, *Commandant of Solitude: The Journals of Captain Collet Barker 1828–1831*, Melbourne University Press at the Miegunyah Press, Carlton, Victoria, 1992.

Shellam, T., *Shaking Hands on the Fringe: Negotiating the Aboriginal World at King George's Sound*, UWA Press, Crawley, Western Australia, 2009.

Shellam, T., 'Manyat's "sole delight": Travelling knowledge in Western Australia's Southwest, 1830s', in D. Deacon, P. Russell and A. Woollacott (eds), *Transnational Lives: Biographies of Global Modernity, 1700–Present*, Palgrave Macmillan, Basingstoke, UK, 2010, pp. 121–32.

South West Aboriginal Land & Sea Council, J. Host with C. Owen, *'It's still in my heart, this is my country': The Single Noongar Claim History*, UWA Press, Crawley, Western Australia, 2009.

About the authors and editors

Murray Arnold is a historian and former farmer from Albany, Western Australia.

Caroline Cartwright is a scientist at the British Museum.

John Carty is Head of Anthropology at the South Australian Museum.

Ian Coates is Head of Collection Development at the National Museum of Australia.

Harley Coyne is a Menang man and Heritage Project Officer, Department of Aboriginal Affairs, Western Australia.

Maria Nugent is a Research Fellow in the School of History, Australian National University.

Gaye Sculthorpe is Curator and Section Head, Oceania at the British Museum.

Tiffany Shellam is Senior Lecturer in History, Deakin University.

Daniel Simpson is a PhD student working in collaboration with Royal Holloway, University of London, and The British Museum.

Alison Wishart is Senior Curator, State Library of New South Wales.

Images

All British Museum photographs are © The Trustees of the British Museum.

Registration numbers for objects are included in the captions. You can find out more about these objects and others in the British Museum collection on the Museum's website at britishmuseum.org.

Notes

1. Kim Scott, *That Deadman Dance*, Picador, Sydney, 2010, p. 69.

2. Kim Scott, 'Not so easy', *Griffith Review* 47, 2014, griffithreview.com/articles/easy accessed 6 August 2016.

3. A. Cunningham, *Journal*, 24 December 1821, 'NSW Colonial Secretary, Special Bundles', Allan Cunningham: Journals and Correspondence. Colonial Secretary's Papers, 1788–1825, Archives Office of New South Wales, reel no. 6034, SZ7.

4. Ibid.

5. Ibid. Shaving Aboriginal people was a common practice during shipboard encounters; see also Shino Konishi, *The Aboriginal Male in the Enlightenment World*, Pickering and Chatto, London, 2012, chapter 2, passim.

6. Cunningham, *Journal*, 24 December 1821.

7. P.P. King, *Narrative of a Survey of the Intertropical and Western Coasts of Australia, Performed Between the Years 1818 and 1822*, vol. 2, John Murray, London, 1827, pp. 130–31.

8. J.S. Roe, 25 December 1821, 'Logbook on board HM brig *Bathurst*, 26 May 1821 – 20 September 1822', Battye Library, ACC 491A/4.

9. Cunningham, *Journal*, 24 December 1821.

10. See B. Buchan, 'Traffick of empire: trade, treaty and *Terra Nullius* in Australia and North America, 1750–1800', *History Compass*, vol. 5, no. 2, 2007, pp. 386–405.

11. Cunningham, *Journal*, 27 December 1821.

12. Ibid.

13. Ibid.

14. T. Shellam, *Shaking Hands on the Fringe: Negotiating the Aboriginal World at King George's Sound*, UWA Press, Crawley, Western Australia, 2009, pp. 184–85.

15. Cunningham, *Journal*, 27 December 1821.

16. J.S. Roe, 'Logbook', 26 December 1821.

17. Cunningham, *Journal*, 27 December 1821.

18. I.S. Nind, 'Description of the Natives of King George's Sound (Swan River Colony) and adjoining country', *Journal of the Royal Geographical Society of London*, vol. 1, 1831, p. 26.

19. King, *Narrative*, p. 144.

20. Cunningham, *Journal*, 25 December 1821.

21. King, *Narrative*, p. 135.

22. Ibid., p. 137.

23. Shellam, *Shaking Hands*, p. 185.

24. C. Barker 1 October 1830, 'Captain Collet Barker's Journal, Fredericks Town, King George Sound', in John Mulvaney and Neville Green, *Commandant of Solitude: The Journals of Captain Collet Barker 1828–1831*, Melbourne University Press at the Miiegunyah Press, Melbourne, 1992, p. 337 (quoted in Shellam, *Shaking Hands*, p. 185); see also J. Carty, 'Kimberley spear points', in *The BP Exhibition. Indigenous Australia: Enduring Civilisation*, British Museum Press, London, 2015, pp. 34–37.

25. *Hobart Town Courier*, 7 September 1832.

26. Shellam, *Shaking Hands*, p. 186.

27. Kew holds at least 30 botanical specimens from King George Sound collected by Alexander Collie and other specimens attributed to 'Collie'. It is unclear whether the latter were collected by Alexander Collie or by the Reverend Robert Collie (1839–1892), another collector of botanical specimens at King George Sound. The renowned curio dealer J.C. Stevens auctioned the Linnean Society specimens after a rationalisation of its collection in 1863.

28. 'Letter from A. Collie to Robert Collie, 22 November 1828 – while in London', National Library of Australia, MA 109.

29. 'Letter from Alexander Collie to Robert Collie, 28 July 1832 – while at Albany', National Library of Australia, MA 109.

30. From an 1836 advertisement by James Drummond, *Magazine of Natural History and Journal of Zoology, Botany, Mineralogy, Geology and Meteorology*, vol. 1, p. 54.

31. W.C. Ferguson, 'Mokaré's domain', in D.J. Mulvaney and J.P. White, *Australians to 1788*, Syme & Weldon Associates, Sydney, 1987, p. 136.

32. An exception was the sealers who came to King George Sound in the wake of Vancouver, and who are recorded as having abducted Menang women.

33. G. Chessel, *Alexander Collie: Colonial Surgeon, Naturalist and Explorer*, UWA Press, Crawley, Western Australia, 2008, p. 139.

34. Mulvaney and Green (*Commandant of Solitude*, p. 246) have speculated that Mokare was the 'Malka' listed in King's King George Sound wordlist.

35. Quoted by N. Green, 'Mokaré (c. 1800–1831)', *Australian Dictionary of Biography*, National Centre of Biography, Australian National University, http://adb.anu.edu.au/biography/mokare-13106/text23711, published first in hardcopy 2005, accessed online 6 October 2016.

36. See Mulvaney and Green, *Commandant of Solitude*; and also South West Aboriginal Land and Sea Council, J. Host, and C. Owen, 2009, 'Inter-cultural connections: Collet Barker and Mokaré 1827–1829', in *'It's still in my heart, this is my country': The Single Noongar Claim History*, UWA Press, Crawley, Western Australia, 2009.

37. 'Letter from Alexander Collie to Robert Collie, 4 August 1833 – while at Albany', National Library of Australia, MA 109.

38. Quoted in Chessell, *Alexander Collie*, p. 148.

39. Collie's entry for 30 April 1831, 'Account of four expeditions in the vicinity of King George's Sound between 27th April and 15th June 1831', in J. Cross, *Journals of Several Expeditions Made in Western Australia, During the Years 1829, 1830, 1831 and 1832*, J. Cross, London, 1833.

40. Collie's entry for 1 May 1831, in Cross, *Journals of Several Expeditions*.

41. Chessell, *Alexander Collie*, p. 147.

42. King, *Narrative*, p. 134.

43. P.A. Clarke, *Aboriginal Plant Collectors: Botanists and Australian Aboriginal People in the Nineteenth Century*, Rosenberg Publishing, Kenthurst, New South Wales, 2008, pp. 86–88.

44. Shellam, *Shaking Hands*, p. 194.

45. Chessell, *Alexander Collie*, p. 152.

46. See T. Richards, *The Imperial Archive: Knowledge and the Fantasy of Empire*, Verso, London, 1993; R.A. Butlin, *Geographies of Empire: European Empires and Colonies c. 1880–1960*, Cambridge University Press, Cambridge, 2009, and J. Gascoigne, *Encountering the Pacific in the Age of Enlightenment*, Cambridge University Press, Cambridge, 2014.

47. B.C. Cohen, 'Alexander Collie (1793–1835)', *Australian Dictionary of Biography*, Melbourne University Press, Melbourne, 1966, pp. 235–36.

48. 'Alexander Collie to Governor Stirling, 24 January 1832', in *Report from Select Committee on Aboriginal Tribes 1837*, Appendix No. 4, p. 130. Copy of a report to Governor Stirling in the appendix to the Report of the Select Committee on Aborigines (British Settlements) with the official report and further evidence, appendix and index (reprinted 1966).

49. For a biography, see Chessell, *Alexander Collie*.

50. For insights into the Scottish Enlightenment, Scottish medical education and the study of mankind, see László Kontler, 'Mankind and its histories: William Robertson, Georg Forster and a late eighteenth-century German debate', *Intellectual History Review*, vol. 23, 2013, pp. 411–29. New research is currently being undertaken by Linda Anderson Burnett and Bruce Buchan.

51. For a survey, see Don Watson, *Caledonia Australis: Scottish Highlanders on the Frontier of Australia*, Random House, Sydney, 1997.

52. Chessell, *Alexander Collie*, p. 11.

53. The relationship between botanical collecting and missionary endeavour is explored in Sujit Sivasundaram, 'Natural history spiritualized: civilizing islanders, cultivating breadfruit, and collecting souls', *History of Science*, vol. 39, 2001, pp. 417–43.

54. Alexander Collie, 'Letters 1828–1835' [transcription of original manuscript], National Library of Australia, MS 109, p. 27.

55. Ibid. p. 36.

56. Collie, 'Letters 1828–1835', pp. 17–19.

57. Chessell. *Alexander Collie*, p. 31.

58. Collie, 'Letters 1828–1835', p. 49.

59. Ibid.

60. For an account of Burnett's career, see David McLean, *Surgeons of the Fleet: The Royal Navy and Its Medics from Trafalgar to Jutland*, I.B. Tauris & Co., London, 2010, pp. 11–21.

61. The history of ethnographic collecting in Australia for the Royal Navy and Haslar Hospital is explored in Daniel Simpson, 'The Royal Navy and Colonial Collecting in Australia', forthcoming PhD thesis, Royal Holloway University, 2017. See also Richard Neville, *A Rage for Curiosity: Visualising Australia 1788–1830*, State Library of New South Wales Press, Sydney, 1997.

62. 'Report from the Select Committee on the Condition, Management and Affairs of the British Museum' House of Commons, 1835, p. 273.

63. William Burnett to William Townsend Aiton, 4 Jan. 1828. Royal Botanic Gardens, Kew, Directors' Correspondence 44/50.

64. For a short, albeit dated, history, see William Tate, *A History of Haslar Hospital*, Griffin & Co., London, 1906.

65. *The Lancet*, vol. 2, 1831, p. 733.

66. See Clarke, *Aboriginal Plant Collectors*.

67. William Balfour Baikie to William Jackson Hooker, 31 May 1855', Royal Botanic Gardens, Kew, Directors' Correspondence 59/17.

68. Alexander Collie, 'Letters 1812–1828', 1 June 1825, State Library of Western Australia, ACC 392A.

69. 'Collie to Hooker, 27 December 1828', Royal Botanic Gardens, Kew, Directors' Correspondence 44/54.

70. Collie, 'Letters 1828–1835', p. 9.

71. Collie sent 852 species of plants from Western Australia to Haslar Hospital Museum between 1829 and 1835. See British Museum, *Return to an Order of the Honourable The House of Commons*, Dated 16 June 1857, British Museum, London, 1857, p. 20.

72. Collie, 'Letters, 1828–1835', p. 48.

73. Ibid. p. 45.

74. Ibid.

75. Cross, *Journals of Several Expeditions*, p. 6.

76. G. Vancouver, *A Voyage of Discovery to the North Pacific Ocean and Round the World 1791–1795*, vol. 1, G & J Robinson, London, 1798, p. 39.

77. M. Flinders, *A Voyage to Terra Australis*, vol. 1, G&W Nicol, London, 1814, p. 58.

78. Ibid.

79. King, *Narrative*, p. 137.

80. *The Australian*, 9 September 1834.

81. M. Hordern, *King of the Australian Coast: The work of Phillip Parker King in the Mermaid and Bathurst 1817–1822*, Melbourne University Press, Carlton, Victoria, 2002, p. 15.

82. Simpson, 'The Royal Navy and Colonial Collecting in Australia'.

83. King, *Narrative*, pp. 135–36.

84. Chessell, *Alexander Collie*, p. 189.

85. D. Starzecka, R. Neich and M. Pendergast, *The Maori Collections of the British Museum*, British Museum Press, London, 2010, pp. 17–20.

86. E.M. Grace, 'Diary transcript Australia-New Zealand (1863–1864)', Knights Sporting Auction, 4 July 2015, Catalogue, Lot 9, http//:shared.knights.co.uk/catalogues/KSA_2015_07/EMG.pdf, p. 28, accessed 6 September 2016.

87. *Sydney Morning Herald*, 31 October 1879.

88. National Library of New Zealand, watercolour sketch by the Rev. A.W. Hands, A 254-050.

89. *Albany Advertiser*, 29 October 1898.

90. *Albany Advertiser*, 30 August 1905.

91. *Western Daily Mercury*, Plymouth, 26 September 1898, republished in *Albany Advertiser*, 3 November 1898.

92. L. Marchant, *France Australe: A Study of French Explorations and Attempts to Found a Penal Colony and Strategic Base in South Western Australia, 1503–1826*, Artlook Books, Perth, 1982, p. 103.

93. 'Colonial Secretary Macleay to Major Lockyer, 4th November, 1826', in *Historical Records of Australia*, vol. 6, pp. 453–54.

94. W.B. Kimberly, *History of West Australia: A Narrative of Her Past, Together with Biographies of Her Leading Men*, F.W. Niven and Co., Melbourne, 1897, p. 64.

95. Mulvaney and Green, *Commandant of Solitude*, p. 403.

96. M. Arnold, *A Journey Travelled: Aboriginal–European Relations at Albany and the Surrounding Region from First Contact to 1926*, UWA Publishing, Crawley, Western Australia, 2015, p. 307.

97. R. Spencer, Letter to Murray, 9/4/1838, copy in Local History Section, Albany Public Library, I.R.S./303 M27.

98. R. Stephens, 'Kendenup, 1840–1940', in *Western Mail*, 30 May 1940.

99. Trimmer to Col. Sec., I.R.S./366M/2, 6/10/1860, Local History Section, Albany Public Library.

100. *Engaging Objects* was funded by the Australian Research Council under the its Linkage Grants Scheme.

101. C.R. Cartwright, 'The principles, procedures and pitfalls in identifying archaeological and historical wood samples', *Annals of Botany*, vol. 116, no. 1, 2015, pp. 1–13.

Acknowledgements

Thanks are due to the Albany Heritage Reference Group Aboriginal Corporation for guiding this publication and associated exhibition in Albany and especially to Harley Coyne for community liaison.

Many individuals working for the related institutions contributed to the project: in the Western Australian Museum, James Dexter, Tanya Edwards, Ross Chadwick, Vernice Gillies and Matt Britton; in the National Museum of Australia, Ian Coates; in the British Museum, Lissant Bolton, Caroline Cartwright, Joanna Fernandes, Thomas Flynn, Jill Hasell, Philip Kevin, Hayley McConnell, Tomasina Munden, Dan Pett and Ian Taylor. We would also like to thank Robert Nichols for his valuable input.

The publication, exhibition and related programs would not have been possible without the support of the Western Australian Museum, the British Museum, the National Museum of Australia, the Art Gallery of Western Australia, the Kerry Stokes Collection, the City of Albany, and the Great Southern Development Commission.

Published 2016 by the Western Australian Museum
49 Kew Street, Welshpool, Western Australia 6106
(Postal: Locked Bag 49, Welshpool DC. WA 6986)
www.museum.wa.gov.au

Designed by Matthew Britton
Printed by Quality Press

National Library of Australia Cataloguing-in-Publication entry

Title: Yurlmun Mokare Mia Boodja 'Returning to Mokare's Home Country': Encounters and Collections in Menang Country / Gaye Sculthorpe and Maria Nugent, editors.

ISBN: 9781925040296 (paperback)

Subjects: Aboriginal Australians—Western Australia—Albany—Exhibitions.
Aboriginal Australians—Western Australia—Albany—History.
Europeans—Western Australia—Albany—Exhibitions.
Europeans—Western Australia—Albany—History.
Albany (W.A.)—History.
Albany (W.A.)—Race relations—History.

Other Creators/Contributors: Sculthorpe, Gaye (author and editor); Nugent, Maria, (editor); Shellam, Tiffany Sophie Bryden (author); Coates, Ian (author); Wishart, Alison (author); Simpson, Daniel Arthur (author); Arnold, Murray (author); Coyne, Harley (author); Carty, John (author); Cartwright, Caroline (author).

Dewey Number: 994.10049915